Video Guide

D1530363

mosaic one

John Dumicich
New York University and Hunter College

The McGraw-Hill Companies, Inc.

New York   St. Louis   San Francisco   Auckland   Bogotá   Caracas   Lisbon
London   Madrid   Mexico City   Milan   Montreal   New Delhi   San Juan
Singapore   Sydney   Tokyo   Toronto

McGraw-Hill

A Division of The **McGraw·Hill** *Companies*

Video Guide to accompany Mosaic One

3 4 5 6 7 8 9 0 QPD QPD 9 0 0 9

ISBN 0-07-050331-1

This book was set in Quark by Chris Boyer.
The editors were Tim Stookesberry and Bill Preston.
The production supervisor was Natalie Durbin.
Quebecor Printing Dubuque, Inc. was printer and binder.

http://www.mhcollege.com

Contents

Preface
to the Third Edition

The Mosaic One Program

The *Mosaic One* program consists of four texts and a variety of supplemental materials for intermediate to high-intermediate students seeking to improve their English language skills. Each of the four texts in this program is carefully organized by chapter theme, vocabulary, grammar structures, and where possible, learning strategies and language functions. As a result, information introduced in a chapter of any one of the *Mosaic One* texts corresponds to and reinforces material taught in the same chapter of the other three books, creating a truly integrated, four-skills approach.

The *Mosaic One* program is highly flexible. The texts in this series may be used together or separately, depending on students' needs and course goals. The books in this program include:

- **A Content-Based Grammar.** Designed to teach grammar through content, this text introduces, practices, and applies grammatical structures through the development of high-interest chapter topics. This thematic approach motivates students because they are improving their mastery of grammatical structures and vocabulary while expanding their own knowledge.

- **A Content-Based Writing Book.** This text takes students step-by-step through the writing process—from formulating ideas through the revision stage. Writing assignments progress from paragraphs to essays, and students write about interesting, contemporary subjects from the sciences, social sciences, and humanities that are relevant to their current or future academic coursework.

- **A Listening/Speaking Skills Book.** This text teaches learning strategies and language functions, while maintaining a strong focus on both listening and speaking. Each chapter includes a realistic listening passage on an interesting topic related to the chapter theme. Short conversations also provide comprehension practice, while a variety of speaking activities reinforce use of language in context.

- **A Reading Skills Book.** The selections in this text help students develop their reading skills in a meaningful rather than a mechanical way—enabling them to successfully tackle other academic texts. The three readings per chapter come from a variety of authentic sources, such as textbooks, magazines, newspapers, interviews, and are accompanied by pre- and post-reading exercises, including skimming, scanning, making inferences, paraphrasing, and group problem solving.

Contents •

Supplemental Materials

In addition to the four core texts outlined above, various supplemental materials are available to assist users of the third edition, including:

Instructor's Manual

Extensively revised for the new edition, this manual provides instructions and guidelines for using the four core texts separately or in various combinations to suit particular program needs. For each of the core texts, there is a separate section with answer keys, teaching tips, additional activities, and other suggestions. The testing materials have been greatly expanded in this edition.

Audio Program for Mosaic One: A Listening/Speaking Skills Book

Completely recorded for the new edition, the audio program is designed to be used in conjunction with those exercises that are indicated with a cassette icon in the student text. Complete tapescripts are now included in the back of the student text. The audio program is now also available for individual student purchase at a special price.

Audio Program for Mosaic One: A Reading Skills Book

This new optional audio program contains selected readings from the student text. These taped selections of poems, articles, stories, and speeches enable students to listen at their leisure to the natural oral discourse of native readers for intonation and modeling. Readings that are included in this program are indicated with a cassette icon in the student text.

Video/Video Guide

New to this edition, the video program for *Mosaic One* contains authentic television segments that are coordinated with the twelve chapter themes in the four texts. A variety of pre- and post-viewing exercises and activities for this video are available in this *Video Guide*.

Mosaic One Video Guide

Rationale

Video Guide to Accompany Mosaic One is a content-based, skill-integrated, project-approach textbook. The exercises and activities in the guide accompany authentic TV segments. The TV segments introduce fresh and topical subject matter into the ESOL classroom, subject matter that is directly related to the twelve chapter themes in the four *Mosaic One* texts. The TV segments are informative and often provocative. The segments serve as vehicles for students to explore the different topics, both through discussion of the factual content of the video clips and through more personalized reactions—how they think and feel about the topics in the video.

Using brief, entertaining video clips is a most productive way to use video in the classroom. Because the TV segments are brief, students can spend more time discussing and reacting to the topics at hand. The video clips do not drain students by requiring them to remember a lot of information. The purpose of the video is to provide a springboard from which students can explore their attitudes toward a subject through summarizing and discussing the content of the video clip. The exercises in the guide aim to elicit the students' own experiences with the subject matter. By exploring their own attitudes, students can expand their own knowledge of the world around them as they expand their fluency in English.

This *Video Guide* is skill-integrated because it contains various exercises and activities to help students to acquire, practice, and fine-tune their language skills. Students first watch the video and summarize the content. Then they listen for discrete items through listening comprehension exercises. They expand their vocabulary through discussion and exercises requiring use of the dictionary and thesaurus. On a more personalized, affective level, students discuss their own feelings about the video clip and topic, and ask and answer their own questions triggered by the video clip. Thus, there is a constant exchange of information, feelings, and questions. This exchange makes the guide highly interactive.

Finally, every chapter of the guide culminates with a project designed to involve the whole learner in his or her own learning. For example, students may have to read, write, listen, draw, go to the library, or observe the space around them in order to create a puppet, collect emergency medical information, or survey a park.

Chapter Organization

Depending on the length or complexity of a particular TV segment, a chapter may have one, two, or three parts, followed by a culminating project. Each part of the video guide corresponds to a specific part of the video clip. Every part of the guide has a pre-viewing activity and various viewing activities.

The **Pre-Viewing Activity** asks students to check words they do not know. They are encouraged to discuss these words with fellow classmates and the teacher.

The **Viewing Activities** include work on **Summary, Basic Information, Vocabulary, Feelings,** and **Questions:**

- **Summary.** Students are first asked to watch a video clip, take notes, and write a summary. Then they interact with one another by reading each other's summaries.

- **Basic Information.** To help students become more familiar with the basic information in the video clip, there are listening comprehension exercises requiring students to answer yes or no to statements relating to the video clip. If the sentence is not correct, students are asked to write the correct information.

- **Vocabulary.** Students build their vocabulary and study skills through different word association exercises. In Part One of every chapter, students are asked to identify a word in each of several groups of words that does not fit the same category as the other words in the group. Then they construct a similar vocabulary exercise of their own, using the words they have just identified. In Part Two, students are asked to match words with opposite meanings. In Part Three, students study word families and write the related forms of different words.

- **Feelings.** After students watch the video clip, they consider a given aspect or feature of the clip and write their response to it. Then, as a group, they discuss their feelings about that aspect or feature.

- **Questions.** Individually, students are asked to write a question about some aspect of what they saw in the video clip. Then, they write their questions on the board so that fellow classmates can offer answers.

The language of the instructions for the exercises and activities is purposely the same throughout the guide. After two or three chapters, students will not have to read the instructions anymore; they will already know them. This predictable format frees the student to focus on the content of the TV segment, and it frees the teacher to pay attention to the students' linguistic output. As a supplemental component of the Mosaic One Program, the video and guide will most likely be used sparingly, perhaps once or twice a week, thus ensuring that the format will not seem repetitive.

An especially exciting feature of each chapter is the culminating project. Each project is different: Some projects are done individually, others are collaborative, and still others require individual work which will be compiled with the work of others.

Teaching Suggestions

Before students watch a video clip, the **Pre-Viewing Activity** invites the class to talk about some key words selected from the TV segment. For each word, focus on the pronunciation, meaning, syllable count, intonation count, stress, and spelling of the words students do not know. There is no need to spend time on words students already know.

When teaching with video, it is important to know your equipment. The television set has volume control for sound and image control for picture. The VCR has a play button, a stop button, a rewind button, a fast-forward button, a slow button, and a pause button. Don't be afraid to use any of them as much as you need to.

With the buttons on the television set and the VCR, you can preview or review video clips by showing the clip with no volume. As a preview activity, for example, when students are viewing the clip for the first time, you can ask students to predict what people are saying and doing. As a review activity, after students have already seen the clip, you can ask students to recall dialogue and events in the clip.

Similarly, you can play the soundtrack without the video picture. Students can be asked to predict what is going on based on the dialogue alone or to use the dialogue to review or reconstruct what has already happened. Additionally, you can ask students to write down parts of the dialogue or individual words they hear that may be unfamiliar to them. When students share their dialogue or words, they are working within the context of the topic of the video clip. You might ask students to organize their words in categories to enhance the retention of lexical items.

The buttons on the VCR can be very helpful in exploiting the exercises and activities in **Viewing Activities.** Show the clips many times. Even after students have completed the basic information comprehension exercises, rewind the clip to go over the information. This will give students enough exposure to the clips to form their own feelings and questions about the topic.

When you press the pause button, you get a still or freeze frame. You can use this still frame to describe a single picture in the video in detail—for example, by focusing on a person's body language or on various background details that may get lost when the video is playing. You can also use this freeze frame to predict action or describe an action in progress. A single frame can also be used to create a story. If you use these techniques, ask students to exchange their work frequently so they get a description or story from other points of view.

Finally, the key to the successful use of this *Video Guide* is to allow students to express their feelings and ask their questions in a supportive environment. Students can disagree with one another, and one opinion does not have more weight than another. And all questions are taken.

CHAPTER one

New Challenges

The Famous People Players: Mentally Handicapped Artists

in this chapter

watch	"The Famous People Players: Mentally Handicapped Artists"
talk	about challenges
create	a puppet

1

Name: _____ Date: _____

PART**one**
Pre-Viewing Activity

exercise 1   Before you watch the video about the Famous People Players, look at the words below. Put a check (✔) beside the ones you do NOT know. Discuss these words with your classmates and teacher.

___ handicapped	___ challenge
___ iridescent	___ frustrating
___ toad	___ tip-toe
___ tableau	___ audience
___ puppet	___ taboo
___ black light	___ segregation

Viewing Activities

Summary

exercise 2   Watch the video clip, "The Famous People Players: Mentally Handicapped Artists" Part One, several times. First, watch the clip and relax. Watch the clip again and take notes. Watch the clip a third time and expand your notes. When you finish watching the video clip and taking notes, organize your notes and write a summary on the lines below.

_____

_____

_____

_____

_____

_____

exercise 3   After you complete your summary, walk around the classroom and show your report to each of your classmates. You, in turn, will read your classmates' summaries.

GROUP
ACTIVITY

Basic Information

exercise 4

Read the following sentences about "The Famous People Players: Mentally Handicapped Artists" Part One. After each sentence, circle YES if the information is correct and NO if you think that the information is not correct. If you circled NO, write the correct information in the space provided.

1. The Famous People Players started 15 years ago.

YES/NO

_____

_____

2. Most of the players are mentally handicapped.

YES/NO

_____

_____

3. The players are invisible on stage.

YES/NO

_____

_____

4. Diane Dupuy is the creator and general manager of the Famous People Players.

YES/NO

_____

_____

5. The theater is based in Montreal.

YES/NO

_____

_____

6. When the Famous Peoples Players first went to New York, they were proud of who they were.

YES/NO

_____

_____

Vocabulary

Below are some words from "The Famous People Players: Mentally Handicapped Artists" Part One. On the line to the right of each word there are four other words. Three of these words belong to the same category as the first word. Circle the word that you think is NOT part of the same category.

1. challenge: difficulty   dare   venture   puppet
2. iridescent: shiny   rainbowlike   audience   shimmering
3. frustrating: baffling   confusing   magic   irritating
4. taboo: tip-toe   prohibition   ban   forbiddance
5. segregation: separation   tableau   apartheid   isolation

On the lines to the left, write down the words you circled in the vocabulary exercise above. Create a similar exercise as the one above. Write three words that have a similar meaning to the word on the left and one word that has an entirely different meaning. You can ask your classmates and teacher for help, and you can use a dictionary or thesaurus. Give your exercise to one of your classmates to complete. Check to see that your classmate circled the appropriate word.

1. _puppet_ : _____ _____ _____ _____
2. _____ : _____ _____ _____ _____
3. _____ : _____ _____ _____ _____
4. _____ : _____ _____ _____ _____
5. _____ : _____ _____ _____ _____

Feelings

1. The player that was interviewed said, "The hardest thing for me on stage is to keep . . . um . . . to keep my energy up, to keep going. Even though sometimes it gets frustrating. Just to keep going." What does she mean by that?

_____

_____

_____

_____

2. Watch the video clip again. This time write about what you feel on the lines below. What are your feelings about the subject matter of the video? Are you interested in the issue? Is it a good idea? Is it a bad idea? Why?

_____

_____

_____

_____

exercise 8

After you finish writing about your feelings, walk around the classroom and show what you wrote to each of your classmates. As a group, talk about what challenges a mentally handicapped person faces.

Questions

exercise 9

Watch the video clip again. On the lines below, write a question that you have about what you saw in the video clip.

_____

_____

exercise 10

Write your question on the blackboard. Each student will read his or her question to the class. Your fellow classmates and your teacher will look to see if the grammar of the question is correct. Ask the class if anyone can help you answer the question.

PART **two**
Pre-Viewing Activity

exercise 1

Before you watch the video about the Famous People Players, look at the words below. Put a check (✔) beside the ones you do NOT know. Discuss these words with your classmates and teacher.

___	inspiring	___	depression
___	coordination	___	achieve
___	imagination	___	odds
___	horrible	___	victory

Viewing Activities

Summary

exercise 2

Watch the video clip, "The Famous People Players: Mentally Handicapped Artists" Part Two, several times. First, watch the clip and relax. Watch the video clip again and take notes. Watch the video clip a third time and expand your notes. When you finish watching the video clip and taking notes, organize your notes and write a summary on the lines below.

_____

_____

_____

_____

_____

_____

exercise 3

GROUP ACTIVITY

After you complete your summary, walk around the classroom and show your report to each of your classmates. You, in turn, will read your classmates' summaries.

Basic Information

exercise 4

Read the following sentences on "The Famous People Players: Mentally Handicapped Artists" Part Two. After each sentence, circle YES if the information is correct and NO if you think that the information is not correct. If you circled NO, write the correct information in the space provided.

1. The Famous People Players have been working for thirteen years to get

their show ready for Broadway.

YES/NO

_____

_____

2. All routines require great coordination and timing.

YES/NO

_____

_____

3. Albert Einstein said the imagination is far greater than knowledge.

YES/NO

_____

_____

4. Diane Dupuy said that the world is in a depression because of money.

YES/NO

_____

_____

5. The newsperson is reporting from Toronto.

YES/NO

_____

_____

Vocabulary

exercise 5

In the left-hand column below, there are some words from "The Famous People Players: Mentally Handicapped Artists" Part Two. Draw a line to match each word with its opposite meaning.

word	opposite
1. routine	defeat
2. victory	rare
3. inspiring	conflict
4. achieve	depressing
5. coordination	fail

Feelings

exercise 6

1. Gordon Billinger, who has been with the Famous Peoples Players for 12 years, said, "We work as a family up there . . . on stage." What does it mean to "work as a family?" Why is working as a family beneficial in getting a job done?

_____

_____

_____

_____

2. Diane Dupuy said: "If the Famous Peoples Players can achieve what they did with their life and get going against all odds, just think what you can do with yours." What about you? What are your challenges?

_____

_____

_____

_____

After you finish writing down what your challenges are, walk around the classroom and show what you wrote to each of your classmates. As a group, talk about your challenges.

Questions

Watch the video clip again. On the lines below, write a question that you have about what you saw in the video clip.

_____

_____

Write your question on the blackboard. Each student will read his or her question to the class. Your fellow classmates and your teacher will look to see if the grammar of the question is correct. Ask the class if anyone can help you answer the question.

PART three
Project

You are going to create a puppet. After you create your puppet, go around the classroom and introduce your puppet to every other puppet in the room. You could introduce your puppet as yourself, or you could create a new personality for your puppet.

The easiest puppet to make is the sock puppet. Follow these directions:

Directions for making a sock puppet

1. Get a clean, new sock. Choose any color you want.

2. Turn the sock inside out.

3. Take the toe of the sock and fold it inward.

4. Sew or staple the right and left sides of the toe.

5. Turn the sock right-side out.

6. Put your hand in the sock until your fingertips touch the end of the sock.

7. Tuck the tip of the sock inward.

8. Put your thumb in the bottom slot of the sock toe and your other fingers in the top slot.

9. Move your fingers up and down to create a mouth for your puppet.

10. Decorate your puppet. Sew buttons for the eyes. Or stick on pieces of colored tape. You can sew, stick on, or staple any other decoration you want. You can color the lips, give your puppet a hat. You can put jewelry on it, a necklace, and/or earrings. You can give it a mustache. Your own creativity will tell you how your puppet will look.

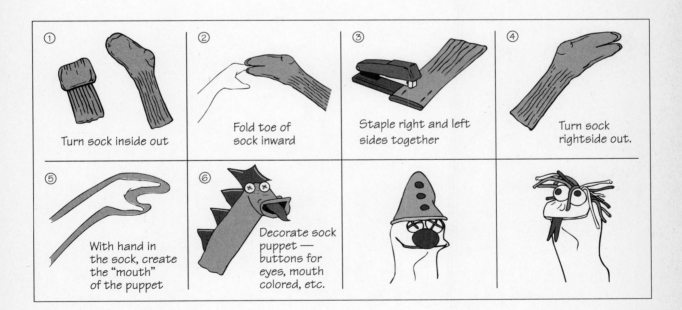

Looking at Learning

School for Success for Both Parents and Children

in this chapter

watch	"School for Success for Both Parents and Children"
talk	about learning
evaluate	your learning style

Name: _____ Date: _____

PART one
Pre-Viewing Activity

exercise 1

Before you watch the video about learning, look at the words below. Put a check (✔) beside the ones you do NOT know. Discuss these words with your classmates and teacher.

___	success	___	network
___	commitment	___	nurturing
___	chattering	___	attitude
___	link	___	structure
___	maintain	___	curious
___	goal	___	community

Viewing Activities

Summary

exercise 2

Watch the video clip, "School for Success for Both Parents and Children," several times. First, watch the clip and relax. Watch the video clip again and take notes. Watch the video clip a third time and expand your notes. When you finish watching the video clip and taking notes, organize your notes and write a summary on the lines below.

_____

_____

_____

_____

_____

_____

exercise 3

GROUP ACTIVITY

After you complete your summary, walk around the classroom and show your report to each of your classmates. You, in turn, will read your classmates' summaries.

Name: _____ Date: _____

Basic Information

Read the following sentences about "School for Success for Both Parents and Children." After each sentence, circle YES if the information is correct and NO if you think that the information is not correct. If you circled NO, write the correct information in the space provided.

1. Part of the goal of the Success Network is to link home, school, and
    community.
    YES/NO

    _____

    _____

2. While the students learn downstairs, the parents are outside.
    YES/NO

    _____

    _____

3. George Frazier is the principal of an elementary school.
    YES/NO

    _____

    _____

4. George Frazier is based in Detroit.
    YES/NO

    _____

    _____

5. The Success Network operates in twenty cities.
    YES/NO

    _____

    _____

6. Money, says Frazier, is the problem in schools.
    YES/NO

    _____

    _____

7. Parents should blame TV for their children's failure in school.

YES/NO

_____

_____

8. Success in school begins with money.

YES/NO

_____

_____

Vocabulary

exercise **5**

Below are some words from "School for Success for Both Parents and Children." On the line to the right of each word there are four other words. Three of these words belong to the same category as the first word. Circle the word that you think is NOT part of the same category.

1. commitment:	obligation	duty	success	pledge
2. link:	unite	connect	join	curious
3. network:	chatter	organization	system	structure
4. nurture:	support	nurse	cultivate	goal
5. curious:	inquisitive	maintain	inquiring	nosy

exercise **6**

On the lines to the left, write down the words you circled in the vocabulary exercise above. Create a similar exercise as the one above. Write three words that have a similar meaning to the word on the left and one word that has an entirely different meaning. You can ask your classmates and teacher for help, and you can use a dictionary or thesaurus. Give your exercise to one of your classmates to complete. Check to see that your classmate circled the appropriate word.

1. _____: _____ _____ _____ _____

2. _____: _____ _____ _____ _____

3. _____: _____ _____ _____ _____

4. _____: _____ _____ _____ _____

5. _____: _____ _____ _____ _____

Name: _____ Date: _____

Feelings

1. George Frazier suggests ". . . keeping your children close to you, keeping a close line of communication, not telling but showing . . ." is the key for success in school. Why is it better for parents to "show" children what to do rather than "tell" them what to do?

   _____
   _____
   _____
   _____

2. When you were in elementary school, were you successful in school? If yes, what do you attribute your success to? If no, why do you think you were not a good student?

   _____
   _____
   _____
   _____

After you finish writing about your feelings, walk around the classroom and show what you wrote to each of your classmates. As a group, talk about what children need to be successful learners.

Questions

Watch the video clip again. On the lines below, write a question that you have about what you saw in the video clip.

_____
_____

Write your question on the blackboard. Each student will read his or her question to the class. Your fellow classmates and your teacher will look to see if the grammar of the question is correct. Ask the class if anyone can help you answer the question.

Name: _____ Date: _____

PART two

Project

Different people learn in different ways. There is the visual learner, the auditory learner, and the tactile learner. A visual learner learns more easily by seeing information; an auditory learner learns more easily by hearing information; and a tactile learner learns more easily through the sense of touch. The Barsch Learning-Style Inventory will help you gain a better understanding of how you learn. (Taken from *English Teaching Forum*, July 1994.)

Barsch Learning-Style Inventory
Jeffrey Barsch, Ed.D.
Revisions by Evelyn C. Davis, Ed.D.

Directions

Place a check (✔) on the appropriate line after each statement, then refer to the scoring instructions on page 18.

	Almost Always	Usually	Sometimes	Seldom	Almost Never
1. I remember more about a subject through listening than reading.	_____	_____	_____	_____	_____
2. I follow written directions better than oral directions.	_____	_____	_____	_____	_____
3. I like to write things down or take notes for visual review.	_____	_____	_____	_____	_____
4. I bear down extremely hard with pen or pencil when writing.	_____	_____	_____	_____	_____
5. I prefer to have an oral explanation of diagrams and graphs.	_____	_____	_____	_____	_____
6. I enjoy working with tools.	_____	_____	_____	_____	_____
7. I enjoy reading graphs, grids, charts, and diagrams.	_____	_____	_____	_____	_____
8. I can tell if sounds match when presented with pairs of sounds.	_____	_____	_____	_____	_____
9. I remember best by writing things down several times.	_____	_____	_____	_____	_____
10. I can understand and follow directions by reading maps.	_____	_____	_____	_____	_____
11. I do better at academic subjects by listening to lectures and tapes instead of reading books.	_____	_____	_____	_____	_____
12. I like to play with coins or keys in my pockets.	_____	_____	_____	_____	_____

Name: _____ Date: _____

	Almost Always	Usually	Sometimes	Seldom	Almost Never
13. I learn to spell better by repeating the letters of the word out loud than by writing the word on paper.	_____	_____	_____	_____	_____
14. I can better understand a news article by reading about it in the newspaper than by listening to the radio.	_____	_____	_____	_____	_____
15. I like to chew gum or eat a snack while studying.	_____	_____	_____	_____	_____
16. I try to remember something by "picturing it" in my head.	_____	_____	_____	_____	_____
17. I learn to spell a new word by tracing the word with a finger.	_____	_____	_____	_____	_____
18. I would rather listen to a good lecture or a speech than read about the same material.	_____	_____	_____	_____	_____
19. I am good at working and solving jigsaw puzzles and mazes.	_____	_____	_____	_____	_____
20. I prefer reviewing written material instead of discussing the subject matter.	_____	_____	_____	_____	_____
21. I prefer listening to the news on the radio than reading about it in a newspaper.	_____	_____	_____	_____	_____
22. I like to obtain information on interesting subjects by reading relevant material.	_____	_____	_____	_____	_____
23. I feel very comfortable touching others (handshaking, etc.).	_____	_____	_____	_____	_____
24. I follow oral directions better than written ones.	_____	_____	_____	_____	_____

When you finish filling out the Barsch Learning-Style Inventory, score the results.
Place the point value of each question on the line next to its corresponding number.
Next, add the points to obtain your preference scores under each one of the headings.

Almost Always	=	4 points
Usually	=	3 points
Sometimes	=	2 points
Seldom	=	1 point
Almost Never	=	0 points

VISUAL		AUDITORY		TACTILE	
#	points	#	points	#	points
2.	_____	1.	_____	4.	_____
3.	_____	5.	_____	6.	_____
7.	_____	8.	_____	9.	_____
10.	_____	11.	_____	12.	_____
14.	_____	13.	_____	15.	_____
16.	_____	18.	_____	17.	_____
20.	_____	21.	_____	19.	_____
22.	_____	24.	_____	23.	_____
total =	_____	total =	_____	total =	_____

Based on the Barsch Learning-Style Inventory, what kind of learner are you?
Do you agree with this evaluation? How is it true? How is it untrue?

CHAPTER three

Relationships

Caring for an AIDS Patient

in this chapter

watch   "Caring for an AIDS Patient"

talk   about being ill

compile   a list of support groups

PART **one**

Pre-Viewing Activity

exercise **1**

AIDS is an acronym. An acronym is a word made up of the first letters of other words. AIDS stands for Acquired Immune Deficiency Syndrome. What does each word in the AIDS acronym mean?

Before you watch the video about an AIDS patient, look at the words below. Put a check (✔) beside the ones you do NOT know. Discuss these words with your classmates and teacher.

___	antibiotics	___	nauseous
___	residue	___	biopsy
___	brain scan	___	lesion
___	MRI	___	healing

Viewing Activities

Summary

exercise **2**

Watch the video clip, "Caring for an AIDS Patient" Part One, several times. First, watch the clip and relax. Watch the video clip again and take notes. Watch the video clip a third time and expand your notes. When you finish watching the video clip and taking notes, organize your notes and write a summary on the lines below.

_____

_____

_____

_____

_____

_____

exercise **3**

After you complete your summary, walk around the classroom and show your report to each of your classmates. You, in turn, will read your classmates' summaries.

Name: _____   Date: _____

Basic Information

Read the following sentences on "Caring for an AIDS Patient" Part One. After each sentence, circle YES if the information is correct and NO if you think that the information is not correct. If you circled NO, write the correct information in the space provided.

1. Antibiotics help the immune system in people with AIDS.

YES/NO

_____

_____

2. Wayne Fisher is a person with AIDS (PWA).

YES/NO

_____

_____

3. Wayne believes that antibiotics help him feel better.

YES/NO

_____

_____

4. Gamma globulin (blood protein rich in antibodies) is taken to boost the immune system.

YES/NO

_____

_____

5. Wayne's condition is constantly improving.

YES/NO

_____

_____

Vocabulary

Below are some words from "Caring for an AIDS Patient" Part One. On the line to the right of each word there are four other words. Three of these words belong to the same category as the first word. Circle the word that you think is NOT part of the same category.

1. nauseous:	squeamish	sick	antibiotics	unwell
2. lesion:	scar	trembling	injury	wound
3. biopsy:	diagnosis	examination	removal	fortunate
4. scan:	browses	survey	healing	checkup
5. residue:	remainder	boost	surplus	leftovers

On the lines to the left, write down the words you circled in the vocabulary exercise above. Create a similar exercise as the one above. Write three words that have a similar meaning to the word on the left and one word that has an entirely different meaning. You can ask your classmates and teacher for help, and you can use a dictionary or thesaurus. Give your exercise to one of your classmates to complete. Check to see that your classmate circled the appropriate word.

1. _____ : _____ _____ _____ _____

2. _____ : _____ _____ _____ _____

3. _____ : _____ _____ _____ _____

4. _____ : _____ _____ _____ _____

5. _____ : _____ _____ _____ _____

Feelings

1. Wayne Fisher feels that being close to nature is very healing. Do you feel the same way? His favorite place is the ocean. What is your favorite thing in nature?

_____

_____

_____

_____

2. Watch the video clip again. This time write about what you feel on the lines below. What are your feelings about the subject matter of the video?

_____

_____

_____

_____

exercise 8

After you finish writing about your feelings, walk around the classroom and show what you wrote to each of your classmates. As a group, talk about the last time you were ill. What was wrong? How did you feel? How did you get better? How long did it take you to feel better?

Questions

exercise 9

Watch the video clip again. On the lines below, write a question that you have about what you saw in the video clip.

_____

_____

exercise 10

Write your question on the blackboard. Each student will read his or her question to the class. Your fellow classmates and your teacher will look to see if the grammar of the question is correct. Ask the class if anyone can help you answer the question.

PART two
Pre-Viewing Activity

Kathy Waldfell is a benefits specialist at the United Federation of Teachers (UFT). A benefits specialist helps people file medical paperwork.

exercise 1

Before you watch the video about an AIDS patient, look at the words below. Put a check (✔) beside the ones you do NOT know. Discuss these words with your classmates and teacher.

_____ nurse   _____ scared
_____ cry   _____ denial
_____ pray   _____ clashing
_____ rely   _____ sublet

Viewing Activities

Summary

exercise 2

Watch the video clip, "Caring for an AIDS Patient" Part Two, several times. First, watch the clip and relax. Watch the video clip again and take notes. Watch the video clip a third time and expand your notes. When you finish watching the video clip and taking notes, organize your notes and write a summary on the lines below.

_____
_____
_____
_____

exercise 3

After you complete your summary, walk around the classroom and show your report to each of your classmates. You, in turn, will read your classmates' summaries.

Basic Information

exercise 4

Read the following sentences about "Caring for an AIDS Patient" Part Two. After each sentence, circle YES if the information is correct and NO if you think that the information is not correct. If you circled NO, write the correct information in the space provided.

1. Wayne and Kathy met in an office.

   YES/NO

   _____
   _____

2. Kathy just helps Wayne file paperwork.

   YES/NO

   _____
   _____

3. Wayne lived with Kathy for over a month.

   YES/NO

   _____
   _____

4. Wayne and Kathy lived together because they got married.

YES/NO

_____

_____

5. Wayne and Kathy never had a fight.

YES/NO

_____

_____

Vocabulary

In the left-hand column below, there are some words from "Caring for an AIDS Patient" Part Two. Draw a line to match each word with its opposite meaning.

word	opposite
1. rely	approval
2. fulfill	laugh
3. heart-warming	ignore
4. denial	abort
5. cry	depressing

Feelings

1. Kathy says she feels emotionally drained. What does this mean? Why does she feel emotionally drained? Have you ever felt this way?

2. Wayne said, "It's very heart-warming to know that somebody cares so much about you that they'll do anything for you." Do you have anyone in your life like that? Who?

_____

_____

_____

_____

After you finish writing about your feelings, walk around the classroom and show what you wrote to each of your classmates. As a group, talk about the people in your life who love you. Who are they? How do they show their love?

Questions

exercise **8**

Watch the video clip again. On the lines below, write a question that you have about what you saw in the video clip.

_____

_____

exercise **9**

Write your question on the blackboard. Each student will read his or her question to the class. Your fellow classmates and your teacher will look to see if the grammar of the question is correct. Ask the class if anyone can help you answer the question.

PART **three**
Project

To help one another through difficult periods, people form "support groups." A support group is a group of people who get together because they have a common concern. They share information, and they console and comfort each other.

You are going to compile a list of support groups for people with AIDS and their friends and families. Get a copy of the *Yellow Pages.* Find the listing for AIDS Help Groups. Make a list of as many AIDS support groups as you can find. When everyone in the class is finished, compile everyone's list to make "A Master List of AIDS Help Groups."

Do Doctors
Prescribe
Too Much?

in this chapter

watch   "Do Doctors Prescribe Too Much?"

talk   about doctors

collect   medical emergency information

PART ONE

Pre-Viewing Activity

exercise 1

Before you watch the video about doctors, look at the words below. Put a check (✔) beside the ones you do NOT know. Discuss these words with your classmates and teacher.

___	treat	___	delay
___	inhibit	___	clot
___	dose	___	prescribe
___	stroke	___	eager
___	FDA	___	investigate
___	potential	___	risk

Viewing Activities

Summary

exercise 2

Watch the video clip, "Do Doctors Prescribe Too Much?", several times. First, watch the clip and relax. Watch the video clip again and take notes. Watch the video clip a third time and expand your notes. When you finish watching the video clip and taking notes, organize your notes and write a summary on the lines below.

_____

_____

_____

_____

_____

_____

exercise 3

After you complete your summary, walk around the classroom and show your report to each of your classmates. You, in turn, will read your classmates' summaries.

Name: _____ Date: _____

Basic Information

Read the following sentences about "Do Doctors Prescribe Too Much?" After each sentence, circle YES if the information is correct and NO if you think that the information is not correct. If you circled NO, write the correct information in the space provided.

1. When treating a heart attack, doctors usually give victims four different drugs.

YES/NO

_____

_____

2. Heart attacks are caused by blood clots.

YES/NO

_____

_____

3. Heparin has known risks of causing bleeding.

YES/NO

_____

_____

4. One in forty patients had a problem with clots reforming.

YES/NO

_____

_____

5. The FDA keeps people informed of the potential dangers of drugs.

YES/NO

_____

_____

6. Researchers want fellow doctors to review data.

YES/NO

_____

_____

Vocabulary

Below are some words from "Do Doctors Prescribe Too Much?" On the line to the right of each word there are four other words. Three of these words belong to the same category as the first word. Circle the word that you think is NOT part of the same category.

1.	inhibit:	restrain	constrain	curb	stroke
2.	dose:	measure	quantity	clot	portion
3.	potential:	possible	likely	probable	treat
4.	risk:	danger	delay	hazard	gamble
4.	eager:	enthusiastic	anxious	avid	prescribe

On the lines to the left, write down the words you circled in the vocabulary exercise above. Create a similar exercise as the one above. Write three words that have a similar meaning to the word on the left and one word that has an entirely different meaning. You can ask your classmates and teacher for help, and you can use a dictionary or thesaurus. Give your exercise to one of your classmates to complete. Check to see that your classmate circled the appropriate word.

1. _____ : _____ _____ _____ _____

2. _____ : _____ _____ _____ _____

3. _____ : _____ _____ _____ _____

4. _____ : _____ _____ _____ _____

5. _____ : _____ _____ _____ _____

Feelings

1. The reporter said, "Too often doctors are eager to report good news. But when it's bad, many hold back on that news for months, even years." Should doctors report their findings to the public as soon as possible, or should they wait?

_____

_____

_____

_____

2. Do you have a personal physician? Do you like your doctor? What makes him or her a good doctor for you?

_____

_____

_____

_____

exercise 8

After you finish writing about your feelings, walk around the classroom and show what you wrote to each of your classmates. As a group, talk about doctors. What qualities make a good doctor?

Questions

exercise 9

Watch the video clip again. On the lines below, write a question that you have about what you saw in the video clip.

_____

_____

exercise 10

Write your question on the blackboard. Each student will read his or her question to the class. Your fellow classmates and your teacher will look to see if the grammar of the question is correct. Ask the class if anyone can help you answer the question.

PART two
Project

You are going to collect medical emergency information.

1. If you attend classes at a college or university, there probably is a medical office where you can go if you need medical attention. Find out where the medical office is and when it's open.

Medical facilities at _____

(name of school)

address: _____

_____

telephone #: _____

office hours:	day	from	to
	Monday	_____	_____
	Tuesday	_____	_____
	Wednesday	_____	_____
	Thursday	_____	_____
	Friday	_____	_____
	Saturday	_____	_____
	Sunday	_____	_____

2. Find the names, addresses, and telephone numbers of the hospitals in your area.

name of hospital: _____

address: _____

_____

telephone #: _____

emergency ward location: _____

emergency ward telephone #: _____

name of hospital: _____

address: _____

_____

telephone #: _____

emergency ward location: _____

emergency ward telephone #: _____

name of hospital: _____

address: _____

_____

telephone #: _____

emergency ward location: _____

emergency ward telephone #: _____

CHAPTER five

High Tech, Low Tech

Forrest Gump,
the Movie
Review

in this chapter

watch	"*Forrest Gump*, the Movie Review"
talk	about movies
write	a movie review

Name: _____ Date: _____

PART**one**

Pre-Viewing Activity

exercise 1

Before you watch the video about *"Forrest Gump,* the Movie Review" Part One, look at the words below. Put a check (✔) beside the ones you do NOT know. Discuss these words with your classmates and teacher.

___	limited	___	twins
___	extraordinary	___	self-made
___	inadvertently	___	idiot
___	wit	___	fame

Viewing Activities

Summary

exercise 2

Watch the first part of *"Forrest Gump,* the Movie Review" Part One, several times. First, watch the clip and relax. Watch the video clip again and take notes. Watch the video clip a third time and expand your notes. When you finish watching the video clip and taking notes, organize your notes and write a summary on the lines below.

_____

_____

_____

_____

_____

_____

exercise 3

After you complete your summary, walk around the classroom and show your report to each of your classmates. You, in turn, will read your classmates' summaries.

Basic Information

Read the following sentences from "*Forrest Gump,* the Movie Review" Part One. After each sentence, circle YES if the information is correct and NO if you think that the information is not correct. If you circled NO, write the correct information in the space provided.

1. Neil Rosen, the film critic for Channel 1, says that *Forrest Gump* is a difficult movie to describe.

YES/NO

_____

_____

2. Forrest Gump is a clever company president from New York City.

YES/NO

_____

_____

3. Nothing ever happens in Forrest Gump's life.

YES/NO

_____

_____

4. Forrest Gump learned how to run fast to avoid getting beat up by the tough kids in school.

YES/NO

_____

_____

Vocabulary

Below are some words from the first part of "*Forrest Gump,* the Movie Review" Part One. On the line to the right of each word there are four other words. Three of these words belong to the same category as the first word. Circle the word that you think is NOT part of the same category.

1. extraordinary:	exceptional	phenomenal	limited	remarkable
2. wit:	intelligence	humor	brains	idiot
3. fame:	process	reputation	notoriety	celebrity

exercise **6**

On the lines to the left, write down the words you circled in the vocabulary exercise above. Create a similar exercise as the one above. Write three words that have a similar meaning to the word on the left and one word that has an entirely different meaning. You can ask your classmates and teacher for help, and you can use a dictionary or thesaurus. Give your exercise to one of your classmates to complete. Check to see that your classmate circled the appropriate word.

1. _____ : _____ _____ _____ _____

2. _____ : _____ _____ _____ _____

3. _____ : _____ _____ _____ _____

Feelings

exercise **7**

Forrest Gump inadvertently attained fame and fortune. What does this mean?

_____

_____

_____

_____

exercise **8**

After you finish writing about your feelings, walk around the classroom and show what you wrote to each of your classmates. As a group, talk about what makes people famous.

Questions

exercise **9**

Watch the video clip again. On the lines below, write a question that you have about what you saw in the video clip.

_____

_____

exercise **10**

Write your question on the blackboard. Each student will read his or her question to the class. Your fellow classmates and your teacher will look to see if the grammar of the question is correct. Ask the class if anyone can help you answer the question.

PART two

Pre-Viewing Activity

exercise 1

Before you watch "*Forrest Gump,* the Movie Review" Part Two, look at the words below. Put a check (✔) beside the ones you do NOT know. Discuss these words with your classmates and teacher.

_____ decade   _____ wisdom
_____ turbulent   _____ fictitious
_____ marvel   _____ interact
_____ ingenious   _____ impact

Viewing Activities

Summary

exercise 2

Watch "*Forrest Gump,* the Movie Review" Part Two, several times. First, watch the clip and relax. Watch the video clip again and take notes. Watch the video clip a third time and expand your notes. When you finish watching the video clip and taking notes, organize your notes and write a summary on the lines below.

_____

_____

_____

_____

_____

_____

exercise 3

After you complete your summary, walk around the classroom and show your report to each of your classmates. You, in turn, will read your classmates' summaries.

Basic Information

Read the following sentences from "*Forrest Gump,* the Movie Review" Part Two. After each sentence, circle YES if the information is correct and NO if you think that the information is not correct. If you circled NO, write the correct information in the space provided.

1. The film spans three decades of American history.

YES/NO

_____

_____

2. Presidents Kennedy and Nixon were on the movie set with Tom Hanks.

YES/NO

_____

_____

3. Forrest Gump knows that he has a great impact on society.

YES/NO

_____

_____

4. Forrest Gump was greatly influenced by his brother.

YES/NO

_____

_____

Vocabulary

exercise 5

In the left-hand column below, there are some words from "*Forrest Gump,* the Movie Review" Part Two. Draw a line to match each word with its opposite meaning.

word	opposite
1. turbulent	real
2. fictitious	inept
3. ingenious	peaceful
4. interactive	bore
5. marvel	solitary

Feelings

exercise 6

Forrest Gump's mother is played by actress Sally Field. Her words of wisdom to her son were, "Life is like a box of chocolate. You never know what you are going to get." What does this mean?

_____

_____

_____

_____

exercise 7

After you finish writing about your feelings, walk around the classroom and show what you wrote to each of your classmates. As a group, talk about *Forrest Gump,* the movie. Did you see it? Did you like it? Why or why not?

Questions

exercise 8

Watch the video clip again. On the lines below, write a question that you have about what you saw in the video clip.

_____

_____

exercise 9

Write your question on the blackboard. Each student will read his or her question to the class. Your fellow classmates and your teacher will look to see if the grammar of the question is correct. Ask the class if anyone can help you answer the question.

Name: _____   Date: _____

PART three
Pre-Viewing Activity

exercise 1

Before you watch "*Forrest Gump,* the Movie Review" Part Three, look at the words below. Put a check (✔) beside the ones you do NOT know. Discuss these words with your classmates and teacher.

___ sensational		___ naive
___ contemporary		___ ethics
___ warmth		___ cast
___ cast		___ pathos

Viewing Activities

Summary

exercise 2

Watch the video clip, "*Forrest Gump,* the Movie Review" Part Three, several times. First, watch the clip and relax. Watch the video clip again and take notes. Watch the video clip a third time and expand your notes. When you finish watching the video clip and taking notes, organize your notes and write a summary on the lines below.

_____

_____

_____

_____

_____

_____

exercise 3

After you complete your summary, walk around the classroom and show your report to each of your classmates. You, in turn, will read your classmates' summaries.

Basic Information

Read the following sentences from the video clip, "*Forrest Gump,* the Movie Review" Part Three. After each sentence, circle YES if the information is correct and NO if you think that the information is not correct. If you circled NO, write the correct information in the space provided.

1. As Forrest Gump, Tom Hanks gave a sensational performance, but the supporting cast was not good.

YES/NO

_____

_____

2. *Forrest Gump* is filled with many laughs.

YES/NO

_____

_____

3. Neil Rosen did not like the film.

YES/NO

_____

_____

Vocabulary

Below are some words from the video clip, "*Forrest Gump,* the Movie Review" Part Three. On the lines provided, fill in the appropriate forms of the word. If the word does not have one of the forms, leave the space blank.

noun	verb	adjective
1. _____	_____	naive
2. ethics	_____	_____
3. humor	_____	_____
4. _____	_____	warm
5. _____	_____	sensational

Feelings

exercise **6**

1. Did you see *Forrest Gump*? Do you agree with the film critic's review?
   Why or why not?

   _____

   _____

   _____

   _____

2. What is your favorite movie? Why is it your favorite?

   _____

   _____

   _____

   _____

exercise **7**

After you finish writing about your feelings, walk around the classroom and show
what you wrote to each of your classmates. As a group, talk about your favorite
movies. What were they about? Why did you like them?

Questions

exercise **8**

Watch the video clip again. On the lines below, write a question that you have about
what you saw in the video clip.

_____

_____

exercise **9**

Write your question on the blackboard. Each student will read his or her question to
the class. Your fellow classmates and your teacher will look to see if the grammar of
the question is correct. Ask the class if anyone can help you answer the question.

PART four
Project

You are going to write a movie review. First, pick a movie you want to write about. It could be your favorite movie, a movie you recently saw, a movie that you did not like, or a movie that influenced you somehow. Write the name of the movie on the line below.

_____

Now write your movie review. Use the following questions as a guideline:

- Did you like the movie or not? Why or why not?

- What was the movie about? Write a plot summary.

- Who starred in the film?

- Were the actors good? Why or why not?

- Would you recommend the film? Why or why not?

When you finish writing your movie review, walk around the classroom and read your classmates' reviews. You, in turn, will read their reviews.

CHAPTER six

Money Matters

Bulls and Bears:
The Stock
Market

in this chapter

watch   "Bulls and Bears: The Stock Market"

talk   about money

list   your credit cards and their interest rates

PART**one**
Pre-Viewing Activity

exercise 1

"Bull" market is a general term that refers to an advancing stock market, one that is making money. "Bear" market is a general term that refers to a market that is slowing down, one that is not making money.

Before you watch the video about the stock market, look at the words below. Put a check (✔) beside the ones you do NOT know. Discuss these words with your classmates and teacher.

____ crumble   ____ require
____ decline   ____ confirmation
____ reverse   ____ accelerate
____ previous   ____ economic
____ bottom line   ____ concern

Viewing Activities

Summary

exercise 2

Watch the video clip, "Bulls and Bears: The Stock Market" Part One, several times. First, watch the clip and relax. Watch the video clip again and take notes. Watch the video clip a third time and expand your notes. When you finish watching the video clip and taking notes, organize your notes and write a summary on the lines below.

_____

_____

_____

_____

_____

_____

exercise 3

GROUP ACTIVITY

After you complete your summary, walk around the classroom and show your report to each of your classmates. You, in turn, will read your classmates' summaries.

Basic Information

Read the following sentences on "Bulls and Bears: The Stock Market" Part One. After each sentence, circle YES if the information is correct and NO if you think that the information is not correct. If you circled NO, write the correct information in the space provided.

1. The commentator announced that the bull market died yesterday.

YES/NO

_____

_____

2. The bull market lasted through a long part of the year.

YES/NO

_____

_____

3. The stock market is in a five-year decline.

YES/NO

_____

_____

4. The commentator said that the decline slowed down during the winters of 1992 and 1993.

YES/NO

_____

_____

Vocabulary

Below are some words from "Bulls and Bears: The Stock Market" Part One. On the line to the right of each word there are four other words. Three of these words belong to the same category as the first word. Circle the word that you think is NOT part of the same category.

1. decline: sink   previous   deteriorate   descent

2. crumble: decay   break down   reverse   decompose

3. accelerate: require   speed   hasten   hurry

4. confirmation: testimony   evidence   proof   concern

exercise **6**

On the lines to the left, write down the words you circled in the vocabulary exercise above. Create a similar exercise as the one above. Write three words that have a similar meaning to the word on the left and one word that has an entirely different meaning. You can ask your classmates and teacher for help, and you can use a dictionary or thesaurus. Give your exercise to one of your classmates to complete. Check to see that your classmate circled the appropriate word.

1. _____: _____ _____ _____ _____

2. _____: _____ _____ _____ _____

3. _____: _____ _____ _____ _____

4. _____: _____ _____ _____ _____

Feelings

exercise **7**

The commentator said that many people are looking for an interest rate cut. What does this mean? Why is an interest rate cut good for consumers?

_____

_____

_____

_____

exercise **8**

GROUP ACTIVITY

After you finish writing about your feelings, walk around the classroom and show what you wrote to each of your classmates. As a group, talk about interest rates. Why do banks charge interest rates?

Questions

exercise **9**

Watch the video clip again. On the lines below, write a question that you have about what you saw in the video clip.

_____

_____

exercise **10**

GROUP ACTIVITY

Write your question on the blackboard. Each student will read his or her question to the class. Your fellow classmates and your teacher will look to see if the grammar of the question is correct. Ask the class if anyone can help you answer the question.

PART **two**

Pre-Viewing Activity

exercise 1

Before you watch the video about the stock market, look at the words below. Put a check (✔) beside the ones you do NOT know. Discuss these words with your classmates and teacher.

____ disconcerting
____ sharply
____ profit
____ estimates

____ token
____ rate
____ retail
____ discount

Viewing Activities

Summary

exercise 2

Watch the video clip, "Bulls and Bears: The Stock Market" Part Two, several times. First, watch the clip and relax. Watch the video clip again and take notes. Watch the video clip a third time and expand your notes. When you finish watching the video clip and taking notes, organize your notes and write a summary on the lines below.

_____

_____

_____

_____

_____

_____

exercise 3

GROUP ACTIVITY

After you complete your summary, walk around the classroom and show your report to each of your classmates. You, in turn, will read your classmates' summaries.

Basic Information

Read the following sentences about "Bulls and Bears: The Stock Market" Part Two. After each sentence, circle YES if the information is correct and NO if you think that the information is not correct. If you circled NO, write the correct information in the space provided.

1. The economic data continues to look promising.

YES/NO

_____

_____

2. New car and truck sales were soft after they had been up sharply for most of the year.

YES/NO

_____

_____

3. Home sales were soft.

YES/NO

_____

_____

4. The commentator claims that things have changed on Wall Street.

YES/NO

_____

_____

Vocabulary

In the left-hand column below, there are some words from "Bulls and Bears: The Stock Market" Part Two. Draw a line to match each word with its opposite meaning.

word	opposite
1. profit	soothing
2. estimates	increase
3. discount	finalizes
4. disconcerting	loss
5. retail	wholesale

Feelings

exercise 6

What does money mean to you? Are you interested in making lots of money? What can money give you?

_____

_____

_____

_____

exercise 7

GROUP ACTIVITY

After you finish writing about your feelings, walk around the classroom and show what you wrote to each of your classmates. As a group, talk about your feelings toward money.

Questions

exercise 8

Watch the video clip again. On the lines below, write a question that you have about what you saw in the video clip.

_____

_____

exercise 9

GROUP ACTIVITY

Write your question on the blackboard. Each student will read his or her question to the class. Your fellow classmates and your teacher will look to see if the grammar of the question is correct. Ask the class if anyone can help you answer the question.

PART three
Project

You are going to make a list of your credit cards and their interest rates. Do you have any of the following credit cards? Place a check (✔) next to the ones you have.

____ Visa
____ Master Card
____ Discover
____ American Express
____ Diners Club
____ department store cards
____ others _____

Do you know the interest rate of the credit cards you have? Look at your credit statements. On the line to the right, write down the interest rate for each card you have.

card	interest rate
Visa	_____%
Master Card	_____%
Discover	_____%
American Express	_____%
Diners Club	_____%
department stores and others:	

_____   _____%
(name of store)

_____   _____%
(name of store)

_____   _____%
(name of store)

CHAPTER seven

Leisure Time

New York
Nightlife Guide

in this chapter

watch	"New York Nightlife Guide"
talk	about what you like to do in your free time
assemble	a tour guide

PART one
Pre-Viewing Activity

exercise 1

Before you watch the video about leisure time, look at the words below. Put a check (✔) beside the ones you do NOT know. Discuss these words with your classmates and teacher.

___ guide   ___ ambiance
___ chic   ___ typical
___ trendy   ___ elegant
___ atmosphere   ___ casual

Viewing Activities

Summary

exercise 2

Watch the video clip, "New York Nightlife Guide" Part One, several times. First, watch the clip and relax. Watch the video clip again and take notes. Watch the video clip a third time and expand your notes. When you finish watching the video clip and taking notes, organize your notes and write a summary on the lines below.

_____

_____

_____

_____

_____

_____

exercise 3

After you complete your summary, walk around the classroom and show your report to each of your classmates. You, in turn, will read your classmates' summaries.

Basic Information

Read the following sentences on "New York Nightlife Guide" Part One. After each sentence, circle YES if the information is correct and NO if you think that the information is not correct. If you circled NO, write the correct information in the space provided.

1. *Seen* is a TV program that tells you about New York nightlife.

YES/NO

_____

_____

2. *Seen* covers nightclubs, discos, and restaurants.

YES/NO

_____

_____

3. *Seen*'s target audience is an older crowd of over 50.

YES/NO

_____

_____

4. *Seen* focuses on the quality of food in restaurants rather than the atmosphere.

YES/NO

_____

_____

5. The nightlife guide in *Seen* starts at 8:00 P.M. and works its way to 6:00 A.M.

YES/NO

_____

_____

Vocabulary

exercise 5

Below are some words from "New York Nightlife Guide" Part One. On the line to the right of each word there are four other words. Three of these words belong to the same category as the first word. Circle the word that you think is NOT part of the same category.

1. guide: escort   handbook   manual   ambiance

2. trendy: chic   fashionable   typical   stylish

3. atmosphere: casual   mood   environment   climate

4. elegant: tasteful   focus   posh   sophisticated

exercise 6

On the lines to the left, write down the words you circled in the vocabulary exercise above. Create a similar exercise as the one above. Write three words that have a similar meaning to the word on the left and one word that has an entirely different meaning. You can ask your classmates and teacher for help, and you can use a dictionary or thesaurus. Give your exercise to one of your classmates to complete. Check to see that your classmate circled the appropriate word.

1. _____: _____ _____ _____ _____

2. _____: _____ _____ _____ _____

3. _____: _____ _____ _____ _____

4. _____: _____ _____ _____ _____

Feelings

exercise 7

Zachary Soreff, the editor of *Seen,* says that the magazine's target is a young market, not like a guide that has an older focus. How would a guide for an older crowd differ from a guide for young people?

_____

_____

_____

_____

exercise 8

After you finish writing about your feelings, walk around the classroom and show what you wrote to each of your classmates. As a group, talk about how leisure time differs for different age groups.

Questions

exercise 9

Watch the video clip again. On the lines below, write a question that you have about what you saw in the video clip.

_____

_____

exercise 10

GROUP ACTIVITY

Write your question on the blackboard. Each student will read his or her question to the class. Your fellow classmates and your teacher will look to see if the grammar of the question is correct. Ask the class if anyone can help you answer the question.

PART two

Pre-Viewing Activity

exercise 1

Before you watch the video about leisure time, look at the words below. Put a check (✔) beside the ones you do NOT know. Discuss these words with your classmates and teacher.

___	research	___	"in"
___	current	___	"out"
___	famous	___	warn
___	hot spot	___	updated

Viewing Activities

Summary

exercise 2

Watch the video clip, "New York Nightlife Guide" Part Two, several times. First, watch the clip and relax. Watch the video clip again and take notes. Watch the video clip a third time and expand your notes. When you finish watching the video clip and taking notes, organize your notes and write a summary on the lines below.

_____

_____

_____

_____

_____

_____

exercise 3

After you complete your summary, walk around the classroom and show your report to each of your classmates. You, in turn, will read your classmates' summaries.

Basic Information

exercise 4

Read the following sentences on "New York Nightlife Guide" Part Two. After each sentence, circle YES if the information is correct and NO if you think that the information is not correct. If you circled NO, write the correct information in the space provided.

1. Zachary Soreff didn't like doing the research for the nightlife guide.

YES/NO

_____

_____

2. The guidebook is updated four times a year.

YES/NO

_____

_____

3. The guidebook sells for $15.95.

YES/NO

_____

_____

4. You can buy *Seen* only in bookstores.

YES/NO

_____

_____

Vocabulary

In the left-hand column below, there are some words from "New York Nightlife Guide" Part Two. Draw a line to match each word with its opposite meaning.

word	opposite
1. current	"out"
2. famous	old-fashioned
3. research	ignore
4. "in"	fossilized
5. updated	unknown

Feelings

How do you spend your leisure time? What do you do on the weekends during the day? Do you go out at night? Where do you go? What are your favorite restaurants, nightclubs, or cafes in the place where you live now?

_____

_____

_____

_____

After you finish writing about your feelings, walk around the classroom and show what you wrote to each of your classmates. As a group, talk about what you do in your leisure time.

Questions

Watch the video clip again. On the lines below, write a question that you have about what you saw in the video clip.

_____

_____

Write your question on the blackboard. Each student will read his or her question to the class. Your fellow classmates and your teacher will look to see if the grammar of the question is correct. Ask the class if anyone can help you answer the question.

Name: _____   Date: _____

PART three
Project

You are going to assemble a tour guide of your city of origin. When everyone in the class has a completed tour guide, collect all the guides in one pile. (Alphabetical order is usually the best way to sequence things.) Find facilities to photocopy the class tour guide. Perhaps you can get it copied at your school. Or you can find out how much it costs at your local photocopy shop and see if the class is willing to chip in on the expense. Then, everyone in class will have a copy of the class tour guide.

To help you assemble your tour guide, answer each question below. You can also include pictures.

Tour guide information:

What is the name of the city or region?

Is it a large or small place? What is its population?

Where is it?

What language(s) do people speak there?

How do you get there from where you are?

What is the approximate fare?

Do you need a passport?

Do you need a visa?

Do you need any special shots?

What kind of clothes should one bring?

What is the currency called?

What is the exchange rate to the dollar?

What are the recommended hotels?

What is the price range for an average hotel room?

What are the recommended restaurants?

What is the price range of an average dinner?

What are the places of interest?

Why are they known?

Why should someone want to see them?

Do you have any personal stories about the place?

CHAPTER eight

Creativity

An Impression
of New York

in this chapter

watch	"An Impression of New York"
talk	about art
go	to a museum

PART ONE

Pre-Viewing Activity

exercise 1

Before you watch the video about American Impressionism, look at the words below. Put a check (✔) beside the ones you do NOT know. Discuss these words with your classmates and teacher.

___ impression   ___ favorable
___ portray   ___ image
___ rectify   ___ ode
___ compete   ___ frame
___ curator   ___ gallery

Viewing Activities

Summary

exercise 2

Watch the video clip, "An Impression of New York" Part One, several times. First, watch the clip and relax. Watch the video clip again and take notes. Watch the video clip a third time and expand your notes. When you finish watching the video clip and taking notes, organize your notes and write a summary on the lines below.

_____

_____

_____

_____

_____

_____

exercise 3

After you complete your summary, walk around the classroom and show your report to each of your classmates. You, in turn, will read your classmates' summaries.

Basic Information

Read the following sentences on "An Impression of New York" Part One. After each sentence, circle YES if the information is correct and NO if you think that the information is not correct. If you circled NO, write the correct information in the space provided.

1. Since the 1970s, Americans have begun to take note of French Impressionism.

   YES/NO

   _____

   _____

2. The exhibition of American Impressionism has 83 paintings at the Museum of Modern Art.

   YES/NO

   _____

   _____

3. H. Barbara Weinberg is the reporter.

   YES/NO

   _____

   _____

4. Weinberg said that the American Impressionists wanted everything to look good.

   YES/NO

   _____

   _____

5. The American Impressionists were inspired by country scenes.

   YES/NO

   _____

   _____

Vocabulary

exercise 5

Below are some words from "An Impression of New York" Part One. On the line to the right of each word there are four other words. Three of these words belong to the same category as the first word. Circle the word that you think is NOT part of the same category.

1. portray:	rectify	represent	depict	describe
2. impression:	imprint	thought	frame	notion
3. compete:	rival	image	vie	contest
4. ode:	poem	lyric	ballad	favorable

exercise 6

On the lines to the left, write down the words you circled in the vocabulary exercise above. Create a similar exercise as the one above. Write three words that have a similar meaning to the word on the left and one word that has an entirely different meaning. You can ask your classmates and teacher for help, and you can use a dictionary or thesaurus. Give your exercise to one of your classmates to complete. Check to see that your classmate circled the appropriate word.

1. _____ : _____   _____   _____   _____

2. _____ : _____   _____   _____   _____

3. _____ : _____   _____   _____   _____

4. _____ : _____   _____   _____   _____

Feelings

exercise 7

There are many styles of painting in the constantly evolving world of art---for example, impressionism, expressionism, realism, cubism, surrealism, modernism, and post-modernism. What is your favorite style of painting? Why is it your favorite?

_____

_____

_____

_____

exercise 8

After you finish writing about your feelings, walk around the classroom and show what you wrote to each of your classmates. As a group, talk about styles of painting. Which is your favorite style of painting? Who are noted artists in that style?

Questions

exercise 9

Watch the video clip again. On the lines below, write a question that you have about what you saw in the video clip.

_____

_____

exercise 10

GROUP ACTIVITY

Write your question on the blackboard. Each student will read his or her question to the class. Your fellow classmates and your teacher will look to see if the grammar of the question is correct. Ask the class if anyone can help you answer the question.

PART two
Pre-Viewing Activity

exercise 1

Before you watch the video about American Impressionism, look at the words below. Put a check (✔) beside the ones you do NOT know. Discuss these words with your classmates and teacher.

___	exhibition	___	burgeoning
___	adopt	___	overwhelming
___	nourishing	___	filter
___	picturesque	___	euphemism
___	edge	___	optimism
___	manageable	___	nostalgia

Viewing Activities
Summary

exercise 2

Watch the video clip, "An Impression of New York" Part Two, several times. First, watch the clip and relax. Watch the video clip again and take notes. Watch the video clip a third time and expand your notes. When you finish watching the video clip and taking notes, organize your notes and write a summary on the lines below.

_____

_____

_____
_____
_____
_____

exercise 3

After you complete your summary, walk around the classroom and show your report to each of your classmates. You, in turn, will read your classmates' summaries.

Basic Information

exercise 4

Read the following sentences on "An Impression of New York" Part Two. After each sentence, circle YES if the information is correct and NO if you think that the information is not correct. If you circled NO, write the correct information in the space provided.

1. The American Impressionists saw the city as a nourishing resource.

YES/NO

_____
_____

2. The time of American Impressionism was a time of political stability.

YES/NO

_____
_____

3. At that time, change was happening rapidly.

YES/NO

_____
_____

4. McSorley's is a bar in New York City that is still in operation.

YES/NO

_____
_____

5. The exhibition on American Impressionism was at the Metropolitan Museum of Art.

YES/NO

_____

_____

Vocabulary

exercise 5

In the left-hand column below, there are some words from "An Impression of New York" Part Two. Draw a line to match each word with its opposite meaning.

word	opposite
1. picturesque	starving
2. nourishing	pessimism
3. burgeoning	wild
4. manageable	unclear
5. optimism	decreasing

Feelings

exercise 6

Do you like going to museums? What is your favorite museum? Why is it your favorite?

_____

_____

_____

_____

exercise 7

After you finish writing about your feelings, walk around the classroom and show what you wrote to each of your classmates. As a group, talk about going to museums. Which museums have you gone to? What was on display?

Questions

exercise 8

Watch the video clip again. On the lines below, write a question that you have about what you saw in the video clip.

_____

_____

exercise **9**

GROUP ACTIVITY

Write your question on the blackboard. Each student will read his or her question to the class. Your fellow classmates and your teacher will look to see if the grammar of the question is correct. Ask the class if anyone can help you answer the question.

PART **three**
Project

You are going to go to a museum. Take a notebook with you. First, take a stroll through the museum and enjoy what it has to offer. Then focus in on a piece of art that appeals to you. Write a critique of that art piece. The questions below will help you with your report.

- What is the title of the art piece?

- Who is the artist?

- What does it look like? Be as specific as possible.

- Why does the art piece appeal to you?

- How do you feel when you look at the piece of art?

CHAPTER nine

Human Behavior

Are Redheads Different?

in this chapter

watch	"Are Redheads Different?"
talk	about personalities
describe	your horoscope sign

PART one

Pre-Viewing Activity

exercise 1

Before you watch the video about redheads, look at the words below. Put a check (✔) beside the ones you do NOT know. Discuss these words with your classmates and teacher.

___	quiz	___	surpass
___	account	___	abundance
___	pioneer	___	discover
___	hyperactive	___	orbit

Viewing Activities

Summary

exercise 2

Watch the video clip, "Are Redheads Different?" Part One, several times. First, watch the clip and relax. Watch the video clip again and take notes. Watch the video clip a third time and expand your notes. When you finish watching the video clip and taking notes, organize your notes and write a summary on the lines below.

_____

_____

_____

_____

_____

_____

exercise 3

After you complete your summary, walk around the classroom and show your report to each of your classmates. You, in turn, will read your classmates' summaries.

Basic Information

Read the following sentences on "Are Redheads Different?" Part One. After each sentence, circle YES if the information is correct and NO if you think that the information is not correct. If you circled NO, write the correct information in the space provided.

1. George Washington, the first president of the United States, was blond.

YES/NO

_____

_____

2. Redheads account for four percent of the population.

YES/NO

_____

_____

3. Dr. Barbara Bartlik claims that redheaded people are pioneers.

YES/NO

_____

_____

4. Dr. Bartlik is a medical doctor.

YES/NO

_____

_____

5. As children, redheads are probably hyperactive.

YES/NO

_____

_____

Vocabulary

Below are some words from "Are Redheads Different?" Part One. On the line to the right of each word there are four other words. Three of these words belong to the same category as the first word. Circle the word that you think is NOT part of the same category.

    1. account: explain   quiz   deem   ascribe

    2. hyperactive: surpass   energetic   vigorous   dynamic

    3. abundance: well-being   prosperity   thriving   discover

    4. pioneer: scout   forerunner   orbit   innovator

On the lines to the left, write down the words you circled in the vocabulary exercise above. Create a similar exercise as the one above. Write three words that have a similar meaning to the word on the left and one word that has an entirely different meaning. You can ask your classmates and teacher for help, and you can use a dictionary or thesaurus. Give your exercise to one of your classmates to complete. Check to see that your classmate circled the appropriate word.

    1. _____: _____ _____ _____ _____

    2. _____: _____ _____ _____ _____

    3. _____: _____ _____ _____ _____

    4. _____: _____ _____ _____ _____

Feelings

Dr. Barbara Bartlik said that redheaded adults are more likely to want to explore. Why does she say this? Are you a redhead? From your experience, do you agree with Dr. Bartlik? Why or why not?

_____

_____

_____

_____

After you finish writing about your feelings, walk around the classroom and show what you wrote to each of your classmates. As a group, talk about people you know who are hyperactive. How do they show this characteristic?

Questions

exercise 9

Watch the video clip again. On the lines below, write a question that you have about what you saw in the video clip.

_____

_____

exercise 10

GROUP ACTIVITY

Write your question on the blackboard. Each student will read his or her question to the class. Your fellow classmates and your teacher will look to see if the grammar of the question is correct. Ask the class if anyone can help you answer the question.

PART two

Pre-Viewing Activity

exercise 1

Before you watch the video about redheads, look at the words below. Put a check (✔) beside the ones you do NOT know. Discuss these words with your classmates and teacher.

____ unique
____ individualistic
____ vibrant
____ mystic

____ attract
____ determine
____ physiological
____ rare

Viewing Activities

Summary

exercise 2

Watch the video clip, "Are Redheads Different?" Part Two, several times. First, watch the clip and relax. Watch the video clip again and take notes. Watch the video clip a third time and expand your notes. When you finish watching the video clip and taking notes, organize your notes and write a summary on the lines below.

_____

_____

_____

_____

_____

_____

exercise 3

After you complete your summary, walk around the classroom and show your report to each of your classmates. You, in turn, will read your classmates' summaries.

Basic Information

exercise 4

Read the following sentences on "Are Redheads Different?" Part Two. After each sentence, circle YES if the information is correct and NO if you think that the information is not correct. If you circled NO, write the correct information in the space provided.

1. Some people think that redheads are more free-spirited than brunettes.

YES/NO

_____

_____

2. Experts say that redheads are different only because of their hair color.

YES/NO

_____

_____

3. Redheads may be physiologically different from people with other hair color.

YES/NO

_____

_____

4. It is certain that redheads are different because of a biological chemical.

YES/NO

_____

_____

Vocabulary

In the left-hand column below, there are some words from "Are Redheads Different?" Part Two. Draw a line to match each word with its opposite meaning.

word	opposite
1. unique	obvious
2. individualistic	detract
3. vibrant	common
4. attract	pluralistic
5. mystic	dull

Feelings

One of the people being interviewed said that redheads are more vibrant and have more fun in life. Do you know any redheads? Does this statement seem to be true?

_____

_____

_____

_____

After you finish writing about your feelings, walk around the classroom and show what you wrote to each of your classmates. As a group, talk about people you know who are redheads. Do they fit the description in the video?

Questions

Watch the video clip again. On the lines below, write a question that you have about what you saw in the video clip.

_____

_____

Write your question on the blackboard. Each student will read his or her question to the class. Your fellow classmates and your teacher will look to see if the grammar of the question is correct. Ask the class if anyone can help you answer the question.

PART three
Project

You are going to describe your horoscope sign and compare it to your personality.

If your birthday is	you are
March 21–April 19	Aries
April 20–May 20	Taurus
May 21–June 21	Gemini
June 22–July 22	Cancer
July 23–August 22	Leo
August 23–September 22	Virgo
September 23–October 23	Libra
October 24–November 21	Scorpio
November 22–December 21	Sagittarius
December 22–January 19	Capricorn
January 20–February 18	Aquarius
February 19–March 20	Pisces

Go to the library and look up horoscope or astrology in an encyclopedia. Write down the characteristics of your sign. How are the characteristics of your horoscope sign similar to your personality? How are they different? Write a report about how you and your horoscope sign are the same or different.

CHAPTER ten

Crime and Punishment

When a
Loved One
Is Murdered

in this chapter

watch	"When a Loved One Is Murdered"
talk	about grief periods
design	a sympathy card

PART one

Pre-Viewing Activity

exercise 1

Before you watch the video about families of murdered victims, look at the words below. Put a check (✔) beside the ones you do NOT know. Discuss these words with your classmates and teacher.

____ victim	____ mourn
____ testify	____ execution
____ stalk	____ floodgates
____ fatal	____ publicity
____ grief	____ appeal

Viewing Activities

Summary

exercise 2

Watch the video clip, "When a Loved One Is Murdered" Part One, several times. First, watch the clip and relax. Watch the video clip again and take notes. Watch the video clip a third time and expand your notes. When you finish watching the video clip and taking notes, organize your notes and write a summary on the lines below.

_____

_____

_____

_____

_____

_____

exercise 3

GROUP ACTIVITY

After you complete your summary, walk around the classroom and show your report to each of your classmates. You, in turn, will read your classmates' summaries.

Basic Information

exercise 4

Read the following sentences about "When a Loved One Is Murdered" Part One. After each sentence, circle YES if the information is correct and NO if you think that the information is not correct. If you circled NO, write the correct information in the space provided.

1. The grief period for someone who is murdered is shorter but more intense than most kinds of deaths.

   YES/NO

   _____

   _____

2. When someone is murdered, friends and family have to deal with the judicial system and the publicity that the case gets.

   YES/NO

   _____

   _____

3. There are many professionals equipped to handle surviving victims of murder cases.

   YES/NO

   _____

   _____

4. The execution system in the United States is slow.

   YES/NO

   _____

   _____

5. There are no support groups for friends and families of murder victims.

   YES/NO

   _____

   _____

Vocabulary

exercise 5

Below are some words from "When a Loved One Is Murdered" Part One. On the line to the right of each word there are four other words. Three of these words belong to the same category as the first word. Circle the word that you think is NOT part of the same category.

1. grief: sorrow   appeal   anguish   heartache
2. stalk: victim   pursue   follow   hunt
3. testify: attest   swear   witness   fatal
4. mourn: grieve   lament   execution   suffer
5. floodgate: publicity   barrier   obstacle   dam

exercise 6

On the lines to the left, write down the words you circled in the vocabulary exercise above. Create a similar exercise as the one above. Write three words that have a similar meaning to the word on the left and one word that has an entirely different meaning. You can ask your classmates and teacher for help, and you can use a dictionary or thesaurus. Give your exercise to one of your classmates to complete. Check to see that your classmate circled the appropriate word.

1. _____ : _____   _____   _____   _____
2. _____ : _____   _____   _____   _____
3. _____ : _____   _____   _____   _____
4. _____ : _____   _____   _____   _____
5. _____ : _____   _____   _____   _____

Feelings

exercise 7

Susan Fisher said that the only people who can help families of murdered victims are people who are going through the same grief. What does she mean by that? How is this true?

_____

_____

_____

_____

Name: _____ Date: _____

After you finish writing about your feelings, walk around the classroom and show what you wrote to each of your classmates. As a group, talk about grief periods. Have you been through a grief period? When? For what reason?

Questions

Watch the video clip again. On the lines below, write a question that you have about what you saw in the video clip.

_____

_____

Write your question on the blackboard. Each student will read his or her question to the class. Your fellow classmates and your teacher will look to see if the grammar of the question is correct. Ask the class if anyone can help you answer the question.

PART two
Project

You are going to design a sympathy card.

An expression of sympathy for the death of a loved one is difficult in any language. To help people express their sorrow at a time of a friend's death, there are sympathy cards. These cards usually have a serene front design and the inside message includes words of comfort for the surviving family members. Go to a card shop and look at the selection of sympathy cards. Then design your own.

CHAPTER eleven

The Physical World

Ocelots: Wildcats in the U.S.

in this chapter

watch	"Ocelots: Wildcats in the U.S."
talk	about pets
survey	a park

PART **one**
Pre-Viewing Activity

exercise 1

Before you watch the video about wildcats, look at the words below. Put a check (✔) beside the ones you do NOT know. Discuss these words with your classmates and teacher.

___ nocturnal	___ environment
___ trap	___ inseminate
___ means	___ captivity
___ habitat	___ costly
___ roam	___ utilize
___ recovery	___ thorn

Viewing Activities

Summary

exercise 2

Watch the video clip, "Ocelots: Wildcats in the U.S.," several times. First, watch the clip and relax. Watch the video clip again and take notes. Watch the video clip a third time and expand your notes. When you finish watching the video clip and taking notes, organize your notes and write a summary on the lines below.

_____

_____

_____

_____

_____

_____

exercise 3

After you complete your summary, walk around the classroom and show your report to each of your classmates. You, in turn, will read your classmates' summaries.

Name: _____ Date: _____

Basic Information

Read the following sentences about "Ocelots: Wildcats in the U.S." After each sentence, circle YES if the information is correct and NO if you think that the information is not correct. If you circled NO, write the correct information in the space provided.

1. A radio collar is the only means of studying ocelots in the wild.

   YES/NO

   _____
   _____

2. Ocelots once roamed a very small area of the Northwest.

   YES/NO

   _____
   _____

3. The ocelot's natural habitat is a thorn forest.

   YES/NO

   _____
   _____

4. Scientists knew that there was a large population of ocelots in the United States.

   YES/NO

   _____
   _____

5. Crossing roads is a big danger for ocelots.

   YES/NO

   _____
   _____

Vocabulary

exercise 5

Below are some words from "Ocelots: Wildcats in the U.S." On the line to the right of each word there are four other words. Three of these words belong to the same category as the first word. Circle the word that you think is NOT part of the same category.

1. nocturnal:	nightly	nighttime	noctivagant	costly
2. habitat:	recovery	environment	home	locality
3. means:	channels	mediums	vehicles	utilize
4. roam:	wander	captivity	meander	gallivant
5. inseminate:	implant	infix	sow	thorn

exercise 6

On the lines to the left, write down the words you circled in the vocabulary exercise above. Create a similar exercise as the one above. Write three words that have a similar meaning to the word on the left and one word that has an entirely different meaning. You can ask your classmates and teacher for help, and you can use a dictionary or thesaurus. Give your exercise to one of your classmates to complete. Check to see that your classmate circled the appropriate word.

1. _____: _____ _____ _____ _____
2. _____: _____ _____ _____ _____
3. _____: _____ _____ _____ _____
4. _____: _____ _____ _____ _____
5. _____: _____ _____ _____ _____

Feelings

exercise 7

Would an ocelot make a good pet? Why or why not? What would make a good pet? Do you have any pets? What kind is it? How do you feel about your pet?

_____

_____

_____

_____

exercise 8

After you finish writing about your feelings, walk around the classroom and show what you wrote to each of your classmates. As a group, talk about pets. What role do pets play in a person's life?

Video Guide to Accompany MOSAIC ONE

Questions

Watch the video clip again. On the lines below, write a question that you have about what you saw in the video clip.

_____

_____

Write your question on the blackboard. Each student will read his or her question to the class. Your fellow classmates and your teacher will look to see if the grammar of the question is correct. Ask the class if anyone can help you answer the question.

PART two
Project

You are going to go to a park and survey the environment. "To survey" means to examine a place very closely. You can survey a park by focusing in on the following categories: *form, function, flora,* and *fauna.*

- To show the *form* of the park, draw a blueprint for the site.

- To state the *function* of the park, write about what the site is used for.

- To list the *flora,* make an inventory of the plants by following these directions:

  1. Look around the park. If you know the names of some plants, write the names down.

  2. If you do not know the name of a plant, take a very close look at it, and answer these questions.

     Is it a tree, shrub, flower, vegetable, or grass?

     What color is it? If it is green, what shade of green?

     What shape is the leaf? You can trace or outline the shape of the leaf on paper.

     If it has a flower, name or describe it.

- To list the *fauna,* make a list of the animals that inhabit the park. When you survey the fauna, you have to be patient and observant. Follow these directions:

     Take a slow, quiet walk through the park. Or, sit quietly on a bench or on the grass. What kinds of birds, insects, and animals do you see? Name them or describe them.

CHAPTER **twelve**

Together on a Small Planet

Venice Is
Worth Saving

in this chapter

watch	"Venice Is Worth Saving"
talk	about your favorite city
construct	a collage

PART one

Pre-Viewing Activity

exercise 1

Before you watch the video about Venice, look at the words below. Put a check (✔) beside the ones you do NOT know. Discuss these words with your classmates and teacher.

___	century	___	drain
___	winding	___	scrubbing
___	neglect	___	polluted
___	disgraceful	___	torrent

Viewing Activities

Summary

exercise 2

Watch the video clip, "Venice Is Worth Saving" Part One, several times. First, watch the clip and relax. Watch the video clip again and take notes. Watch the video clip a third time and expand your notes. When you finish watching the video clip and taking notes, organize your notes and write a summary on the lines below.

_____

_____

_____

_____

_____

_____

exercise 3

After you complete your summary, walk around the classroom and show your report to each of your classmates. You, in turn, will read your classmates' summaries.

Name: _____   Date: _____

Basic Information

Read the following sentences about "Venice Is Worth Saving" Part One. After each sentence, circle YES if the information is correct and NO if you think that the information is not correct. If you circled NO, write the correct information in the space provided.

1. For centuries, Venetians have lived on the water.

YES/NO

_____

_____

2. Venice is situated on the Mediterranean Sea.

YES/NO

_____

_____

3. Venice's environmental problems are handled very efficiently by the local authorities.

YES/NO

_____

_____

4. Canals are cleaned every decade.

YES/NO

_____

_____

5. Polluted water is the only problem in Venice.

YES/NO

_____

_____

Vocabulary

Below are some words from "Venice Is Worth Saving" Part One. On the line to the right of each word there are four other words. Three of these words belong to the same category as the first word. Circle the word that you think is NOT part of the same category.

1. winding: meandering   serpentine   snaky   scrubbing

2. neglect: forget   polluted   disregard   overlook

3. disgraceful: torrent   shameful   shoddy   bad

On the lines to the left, write down the words you circled in the vocabulary exercise above. Create a similar exercise as the one above. Write three words that have a similar meaning to the word on the left and one word that has an entirely different meaning. You can ask your classmates and teacher for help, and you can use a dictionary or thesaurus. Give your exercise to one of your classmates to complete. Check to see that your classmate circled the appropriate word.

1. _____: _____ _____ _____ _____

2. _____: _____ _____ _____ _____

3. _____: _____ _____ _____ _____

Feelings

Venetians have lived on the water for centuries. What do you think it is like to live on the water?

_____

_____

_____

_____

After you finish writing about your feelings, walk around the classroom and show what you wrote to each of your classmates. As a group, talk about places where you would like to live. Would you like to live on the water? In the mountains? The desert? Somewhere else? Why?

Questions

exercise **9**

Watch the video clip again. On the lines below, write a question that you have about what you saw in the video clip.

_____

_____

exercise **10**

GROUP ACTIVITY

Write your question on the blackboard. Each student will read his or her question to the class. Your fellow classmates and your teacher will look to see if the grammar of the question is correct. Ask the class if anyone can help you answer the question.

PART **two**

Pre-Viewing Activity

exercise **1**

Before you watch the video about Venice, look at the words below. Put a check (✔) beside the ones you do NOT know. Discuss these words with your classmates and teacher.

___	resident	___	sink
___	restore	___	flow
___	toll	___	pump
___	corrosive		

Viewing Activities

Summary

exercise **2**

Watch the video clip, "Venice Is Worth Saving" Part Two, several times. First, watch the clip and relax. Watch the video clip again and take notes. Watch the video clip a third time and expand your notes. When you finish watching the video clip and taking notes, organize your notes and write a summary on the lines below.

_____

_____

_____

_____

_____

_____

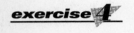

After you complete your summary, walk around the classroom and show your report to each of your classmates. You, in turn, will read your classmates' summaries.

Basic Information

Read the following sentences about "Venice Is Worth Saving" Part Two. After each sentence, circle YES if the information is correct and NO if you think that the information is not correct. If you circled NO, write the correct information in the space provided.

1. Bob Guthrie lives in Venice all year-round.

YES/NO

_____

_____

2. After World War II, the city sank about two feet.

YES/NO

_____

_____

3. As the city sinks lower, high tide flooding is more frequent.

YES/NO

_____

_____

4. Corrosive salt water is crumbling old buildings.

YES/NO

_____

_____

5. All of the money to save Venice comes from the Italian government.

YES/NO

_____

_____

Vocabulary

exercise **5**

In the left-hand column below, there are some words from "Venice Is Worth Saving" Part Two. Draw a line to match each word with its opposite meaning.

word		opposite
1. resident		float
2. corrosive		destroy
3. restore		tourist
4. flow		protective
5. sink		clog

Feelings

exercise **6**

Bob Guthrie says that Venice is a museum. He suggests charging a toll to get into the city. How is Venice a museum? Is charging a fee to get into the city a good idea? What is your favorite city? Should the local authorities charge a fee to enter it?

_____

_____

_____

_____

exercise **7**

After you finish writing about your feelings, walk around the classroom and show what you wrote to each of your classmates. As a group, talk about your favorite city.

Questions

exercise **8**

Watch the video clip again. On the lines below, write a question that you have about what you saw in the video clip.

_____

_____

exercise **9**

Write your question on the blackboard. Each student will read his or her question to the class. Your fellow classmates and your teacher will look to see if the grammar of the question is correct. Ask the class if anyone can help you answer the question.

PART three
Project

You are going to construct a collage of your favorite city. A collage is an artistic composition of pieces of paper, plain or from printed publications, pasted together. This project can be a tourist view of the city, or how you feel about the city.

Here is an example of a collage of San Francisco:

Answer Key
Answers to Basic Information and Vocabulary Exercises

CHAPTER one

PART ONE

Basic Information: Exercise 4, p. 3
1. No   The company is **over 20 years old**.
2. Yes
3. Yes
4. No   Diane Dupuy is **the creator** of the Famous People Players.
5. No   The theater is based in **Toronto**.
6. No   They were **afraid.** They did not think people would like them.

Vocabulary: Exercise 5, p. 4
1. puppet
2. audience
3. magic
4. tip-toe
5. tableau

PART TWO

Basic Information: Exercise 4, pp. 6–7
1. No   The Famous People Players have been working for **three** years to get their show ready for Broadway.
2. Yes
3. Yes
4. No   Diane Dupuy said that the world is in a depression because **nobody knows how to dream anymore.**
5. No   The newsperson is reporting from **Manhattan**.

Vocabulary: Exercise 5, p. 7
1. routine/rare
2. victory/defeat
3. inspiring/depressing
4. achieve/fail
5. coordination/conflict

CHAPTER two

PART ONE

Basic Information: Exercise 4, pp. 13–14
1. Yes
2. No   **The parents are upstairs.**
3. No   George Frazier is **the owner of the Success Network.**
4. No   George Frazier is based in **Cleveland.**
5. No   The Success Network operates in **a dozen** cities.
6. No   Focus on making sure that your child is **given love, attention, support, nurturing, and closeness** that only a parent can give a child.
7. No   Parents should **not** blame TV for their children's failure in school.
8. No   Success in school begins with **an attitude.**

Vocabulary: Exercise 5, p. 14
1. success
2. curious
3. chatter
4. goal
5. maintain

CHAPTER three

PART ONE

Basic Information: Exercise 4, p. 21
1. No   Antibiotics do **not** seem to help people with AIDS.
2. Yes
3. No   Wayne believes that antibiotics make him feel **nauseous.**
4. Yes
5. No   Wayne's condition is **not** constantly improving.

Vocabulary: Exercise 5, p. 22
1. antibiotics
2. trembling
3. fortunate
4. healing
5. boost

PART TWO

Basic Information: Exercise 4, pp. 24–25
1. Yes
2. No Kathy helps Wayne file paperwork **and cooks for him/takes care of him.**
3. Yes
4. No Wayne and Kathy lived together because **he was sick and she was taking care of him.**
5. No **At times** there would be bitter fights.

Vocabulary: Exercise 5, p. 25
1. rely/ignore
2. fulfill/abort
3. heart-warming/depressing
4. denial/approval
5. cry/laugh

CHAPTER four

PART ONE

Basic Information: Exercise 4, p. 29
1. No Doctors usually give heart attack victims **two** different drugs.
2. Yes
3. Yes
4. No **One in twenty or one in ten patients** had a problem with clots reforming.
5. Yes
6. Yes

Vocabulary: Exercise 5, p. 30
1. stroke
2. clot
3. treat
4. delay
5. prescribe

CHAPTER five

PART ONE

Basic Information: Exercise 4, p. 35
1. Yes
2. No Forrest Gump is **a slow-talking, slow-witted Southerner.**
3. No **Extraordinary things** keep happening to him.
4. Yes

Vocabulary: Exercise 5, p. 35
1. limited
2. idiot
3. process

PART TWO

Basic Information: Exercise 4, p. 38
1. No The film spans **four** decades of American history.
2. No Presidents Kennedy and Nixon were **not** on the movie set with Tom Hanks.
3. No Forrest Gump does **not** know that he has great impact on society.
4. No Forrest Gump was greatly influenced by his **mother.**

Vocabulary: Exercise 5, p. 38
1. turbulent/peaceful
2. fictitious/real
3. ingenious/inept
4. interactive/solitary
5. marvel/bore

PART THREE

Basic Information: Exercise 4, p. 41
1. No **The supporting cast was also very good.**
2. Yes
3. No Neil Rosen **liked the film very much.**

Vocabulary: Exercise 5, p. 41

noun	verb	adjective
1. naiveness/naiveté	_____	naive
2. ethics	_____	ethical
3. humor	to humor	humorous
4. warmth	to warm	warm
5. sensation	sensationalize	sensational

CHAPTER six

PART ONE

Basic Information: Exercise 4, p. 47
1. Yes
2. Yes
3. No The Stock Market is in a **three**-year decline.
4. No The commentator said that the decline **may accelerate** during the winters of 1992 and 1993.

Vocabulary: Exercise 5, p. 47
1. previous
2. reverse
3. require
4. concern

PART TWO

Basic Information: Exercise 4, p. 50
1. No   The economic data looks **disconcerting.**
2. Yes
3. Yes
4. Yes

Vocabulary: Exercise 5, p. 50
1. profit/loss
2. estimates/finalizes
3. discount/increase
4. disconcerting/soothing
5. retail/wholesale

CHAPTER seven

PART ONE

Basic Information: Exercise 4, p. 55
1. No   *Seen* is a **book** that tells you about New York nightlife.
2. Yes
3. No   *Seen*'s target audience is a **young** crowd.
4. No   *Seen* focuses on **atmosphere.**
5. No   The Nightlife Guide starts at 8:00 P.M. and works its way to **10:30** A.M.

Vocabulary: Exercise 5, p. 56
1. ambiance
2. typical
3. casual
4. focus

PART TWO

Basic Information: Exercise 4, pp. 58–59
1. No   Zachary Soreff **didn't mind** doing the research for the nightlife guide.
2. No   The guidebook is updated **at least two times a year.**
3. No   The guidebook sells for **$8.95.**
4. No   You can buy *Seen* in bookstores **or by telephone.**

Vocabulary: Exercise 5, p. 59
1. current/old-fashioned
2. famous/unknown
3. research/ignore
4. "in"/"out"
5. updated/fossilized

CHAPTER eight

PART ONE

Basic Information: Exercise 4, p. 63
1. No   Since the 1970s, Americans have begun to take notice **of the stepchild of French Impressionism: American Impressionism.**

2. No   The exhibition of American Impressionism has 83 paintings at the **Metropolitan Museum of Art.**
3. No   H. Barbara Weinberg is the **curator of the American wing of the Metropolitan Museum of Art.**
4. Yes
5. No   The American Impressionists were inspired by **the streets of New York.**

Vocabulary: Exercise 5, p. 64
1. rectify
2. frame
3. image
4. favorable

PART TWO

Basic Information: Exercise 4, pp. 66–67
1. Yes
2. No   The time of American Impressionism was an **uncertain** political time.
3. Yes
4. Yes
5. Yes

Vocabulary: Exercise 5, p. 67
1. picturesque/unclear
2. nourishing/starving
3. burgeoning/decreasing
4. manageable/wild
5. optimism/pessimism

CHAPTER nine

PART ONE

Basic Information: Exercise 4, p. 71
1. No   George Washington was a **redhead.**
2. No   Redheads account for **two** percent of the population.
3. Yes
4. No   Dr. Bartlik is a **psychiatrist.**
5. Yes

Vocabulary: Exercise 5, p. 72
1. quiz
2. surpass
3. discover
4. orbit

PART TWO

Basic Information: Exercise 4, p. 74
1. Yes
2. No   Experts say that redheads are **not** any different because of their hair color.
3. Yes
4. No   It is **not** certain that redheads are different because of a biological chemical.

Vocabulary: Exercise 5, p. 75

1. unique/common
2. individualistic/pluralistic
3. vibrant/dull
4. attract/detract
5. mystic/obvious

CHAPTER ten

PART ONE

Basic Information: Exercise 4, p. 79

1. No   The grief period for someone who is murdered is **longer** than most kinds of deaths.
2. Yes
3. No   There are **not** many professionals equipped to handle surviving victims of murder cases.
4. Yes
5. No   **There are** support groups for friends and families of murder victims.

Vocabulary: Exercise 5, p. 80

1. appeal
2. victim
3. fatal
4. execution
5. publicity

CHAPTER eleven

PART ONE

Basic Information: Exercise 4, p. 85

1. Yes
2. No   Ocelots once roamed a **large area** of the United States, **from Arizona to Louisiana.**
3. Yes
4. No   Scientists were **not** sure that there was a large population of ocelots in the United States.
5. Yes

Vocabulary: Exercise 5, p. 86

1. costly
2. recovery
3. utilize
4. captivity
5. thorn

CHAPTER twelve

PART ONE

Basic Information: Exercise 4, p. 91

1. Yes
2. No   Venice is situated on the **Adriatic** Sea.
3. No   Venice's environmental problems are **not** handled efficiently by the local authorities.
4. No   Canals **were** cleaned every decade. **They have not been cleaned for 30 years.**
5. No   Venice's other problems **include frequent flooding, air pollution, a torrent of 6 million tourists a year.**

Vocabulary: Exercise 5, p. 92

1. scrubbing
2. polluted
3. torrent

PART TWO

Basic Information: Exercise 4, p. 94

1. No   Bob Guthrie is **a part-time resident** of Venice.
2. No   After World War II, the city sank about **a** foot.
3. Yes
4. Yes
5. No   Money to save Venice comes from **individuals.**

Vocabulary: Exercise 5, p. 95

1. resident/tourist
2. corrosive/protective
3. restore/destroy
4. flow/clog
5. sink/float